WATERLOO SCHOOL LIBRARY

W9-COL-834

MIND CONTROL

OTHER BOOKS BY MELVIN BERGER

Computers in Your Life
Enzymes in Action
The New Earth Book: Our Changing Planet

Scientists at Work Series

Animal Hospital
Consumer Protection Labs
Exploring the Mind and Brain
Medical Center Lab
Oceanography Lab
Police Lab
Sports Medicine

WATERLOO HIGH SCHOOL LIBRARY
1464 INDUSTRY RD.
ATWATER, OHIO 44201

Mind
Control

Melvin
Berger

Thomas Y. Crowell   New York

155.2
BER

Mind Control
Copyright © 1985 by Melvin Berger
All rights reserved. No part of this book may be
used or reproduced in any manner whatsoever without
written permission except in the case of brief quotations
embodied in critical articles and reviews. Printed in
the United States of America. For information address
Thomas Y. Crowell Junior Books, 10 East 53rd Street,
New York, N.Y. 10022.

Library of Congress Cataloging in Publication Data
Berger, Melvin.
  Mind control.

  Bibliography: p.
  Includes index.
  Summary: Describes types of mind control such as
cult conversion, hypnosis, prefrontal lobotomies, brainwashing, and electric shock treatment, some of which are
extremely controversial, especially when applied against
one's will.
  1. Behavior modification—Juvenile literature.
2. Brainwashing—Juvenile literature.   3. Hypnotism—
Juvenile literature.   [1. Behavior modification.
2. Brainwashing.   3. Hypnotism]   I. Title.
BF637.B4B48   1985   155.2'5   82-46004
ISBN 0-690-04348-1
ISBN 0-690-04349-X (lib. bdg.)

Designed by Al Cetta
 2 3 4 5 6 7 8 9 10

CONTENTS

MIND CONTROL

CHAPTER 1.

INTRODUCTION TO MIND CONTROL

Mind Control: The power to direct another
person's, or one's own, thoughts, beliefs,
emotions, judgments, perceptions, and behavior.

Carl was bright, talented, good-looking, and well edu-
cated. Yet he felt lost in New York City. After nearly
a year of looking for work as an actor, he was completely discouraged. The only jobs he could find were
as a part-time waiter and as a helper on a moving van.
He was thinking of giving up and going back home to
Alabama.

A pretty young woman sat down next to Carl on a
bus one morning. She struck up a conversation with
him, and seemed to be sincerely interested in his problems. After Carl told her his story, she invited him to
meet her friends at a church gathering that evening.

When Carl showed up, she introduced him to the

others. They all seemed eager and willing to take Carl into their circle. Everyone was happy, friendly, and wholesome. They exuded a feeling of warmth and a sense of community. Again and again they invited Carl to become a member and move into their large house.

Before the evening was over, Carl decided to join the group. In return for giving him room and board, they only asked that he help out around the house. They also asked him to donate his clothes, personal possessions, and even the few dollars he had saved up, to the church.

From then on, Carl was busy all the time. Between the chores around the house and daily prayer meetings and lectures, he had no time for himself. When he spoke about looking for acting jobs, the group members put him off, saying he would do it next week or the week after. A few times Carl questioned the group's beliefs, and was either ignored or answered with evasions and lies. When he confessed to someone that he was thinking of moving out, he was made to feel so guilty and ungrateful that he never brought the idea up again.

Carl's parents met with him about one month later. They hardly recognized him. He was quiet and withdrawn. His replies to their questions about his daily activities and future plans were dull and uninformative. He shrugged off their attempts to discuss the church group. Instead, he talked to them of the sin and vice in their lives. His parents had the uncomfortable feeling that they no longer knew their own son.

Further attempts to meet with Carl, the parents found, were very difficult. He never returned their calls or answered their letters. The first time they showed up at the church house, they were turned away. The next time, they were threatened with bodily harm. After a year they gave up. About two years later they learned that Carl had married a woman within the church. They had been sent to Oregon to live.

Dr. Paul is an American physician who was working with a missionary group in the Far East. A new government came to power in the country where he was serving. The leaders did not approve of the missionaries' activities. They denounced the group and attacked the leaders. When Dr. Paul objected to their methods, he was arrested.

Dr. Paul was kept isolated in a small, dark, foul-smelling prison cell. Day after day he didn't see or hear another human being. His daily rations of rice, bread, and watery soup arrived through a slot in the door.

After a while, Dr. Paul did not know whether it was

day or night. He was unable to think clearly. He began to see strange and frightening visions. At times his body shook uncontrollably.

One morning, a guard took Dr. Paul to be questioned by two officials. The men pressed him to confess to taking part in terrorist activities against the government. When Dr. Paul refused, they punched and slapped him. After a few hours of verbal and physical abuse, they ordered him back to his cell.

From then on, the interviews with the officials became more and more frequent. During one long session, Dr. Paul was queried and accused for five hours without pause. For the first time, he began to doubt himself: Had he committed some of the antisocial acts for which he was being blamed? He could no longer be sure. The questioners seemed to know everything about him.

That is when Dr. Paul confessed to a long list of crimes against the state. He named several of his friends at the mission as enemies of the ruling party. And he signed a document that detailed all the crimes of which he was guilty.

After this confession, Dr. Paul was given a warm shower and served a tasty dinner. His captives moved him to a cell with a window. Twice daily, after breakfast and lunch, he was allowed to exercise in the prison yard.

Not long after, Dr. Paul was released. At a press conference, he praised the new government and applauded their efforts to help the populace. Outside agitators, such as missionaries, he said, are trying to undermine the legitimate people's government. "Let them be punished severely!" he shouted.

About once a month Betty, age twenty-five, used to have an overwhelming desire for alcohol. Once she started drinking, she found it impossible to stop. Usually, she ended up completely drunk. In this state, she could not control her temper. Twice she was arrested for fighting and attacking others. One time she was almost killed in a barroom brawl.

Betty's family finally convinced her to enter a hospital for treatment. A psychiatrist met with her three times a week. With his help, she was able to recall her very first drinking experiences in high school. Together, Betty and the doctor tried to uncover the source of her intense desire for alcohol. She recalled that she started drinking to keep up with some older friends whom she admired. Then, after graduation, she found that every once in a while she wanted to get drunk just because it made her feel good. And from then on it just grew worse and worse.

Meanwhile, a second doctor worked with Betty in another way. This psychiatrist instructed Betty to look through a set of pictures. Each time she came to a photo of someone taking a drink of alcohol, she got a mild, but painful, electric shock in her arm. After several weeks of this treatment, just the sight of someone drinking made Betty grimace. She acted as though she was getting a shock, even when she wasn't.

After six months or so, Betty no longer craved alcohol. She was released from the hospital. Days, weeks, months, and finally years passed without her drinking a drop of alcohol.

Mr. Burns taught high school mathematics. He was a short, thin man who always moved rapidly with quick, jerky motions. Often his hands trembled uncontrollably. Sometimes he spoke so fast that his students could not understand what he was saying. Although the students liked Mr. Burns, they all agreed that he was far too nervous.

Then, gradually, the math teacher's behavior began to change. He became calmer and more relaxed. His movements and speech slowed down. There was an improvement in his appearance. He even gained some weight.

A fellow teacher asked Mr. Burns what brought about these changes. Mr. Burns told him about a group that he had joined. The members followed the teachings of a spiritual leader in India. From this group, he said, he had learned special ways to discipline his mind and body. He memorized certain prayers, which he repeated several times a day. Also, he performed a set of exercises at home every evening.

A smile came over Mr. Burns' face as he described the calm, peaceful feelings he enjoyed at the meetings and while reciting the prayers or doing the exercises. Beautiful visions, he said, came to his mind. He heard lovely, serene music, and saw colors and shapes that he could not tell about in words. "Sometimes," he went on, "I lose all awareness of my body and feel as though I am floating through the air. I am now master of my own body and mind," he said. "What greater goal can anyone achieve?"

At first, these incidents may strike you as unrelated. But there is one way in which they are all the same. They are all examples of dramatic changes brought about through the application of mind-control techniques.

Each example shows that our thoughts and beliefs, our emotions and feelings, our perceptions and our actions, can be shifted and altered. These changes may occur in any number of different ways:

Carl was led to become a part of the church organization by a combination of group pressure, separation from friends and family, a busy schedule with no time to reflect, and the constant round of prayer meetings and lectures.

Dr. Paul's transformation came about as a result of being deprived of all human contact and of many of the necessities of life. He was made completely dependent on his captors, and finally accepted their doctrines in order to survive.

Betty's destructive alcoholism was reversed in two ways—by gaining insights into the root causes of her drinking, and by building up extremely unpleasant associations with alcohol.

And Mr. Burns gained control of his nervousness and anxiety through a regimen of prayer and exercises that affected his perceptions and thought processes.

For good or evil, mind control is not a new concept. It dates back to the very beginning of history. Since primitive times, authorities have used whips and clubs, chains and prisons to impose their beliefs and values on others. In addition, people themselves have long used alcohol and other chemical substances, frenzied dancing and magical rituals, to alter their own ways of thinking and feeling.

Although techniques of mind control can be traced far back in time, some remarkable changes have occurred very recently. Advances in our scientific understanding of the human mind and brain, refinement of electronic technology and computers, and the development of new and more powerful mind drugs have vastly increased the power of mind control. In our time, too, has come an increased willingness to use these techniques. The result is that mind control is more effective and more widespread than ever before. It is a familiar part of almost everyone's experience.

George Orwell's well-known novel *1984*, published in 1949, tells an imaginary, futuristic story of a country that is dominated by Big Brother. Big Brother maintains his power over the entire population by using the most advanced mind-control methods that the author could imagine when he wrote the book. It is interesting to compare his vision of mind control with the reality and the potential of mind control today. The possible uses of mind control in our age go far beyond his fictional account. Given the right conditions, a real Big Brother actually could capture the minds and change the behaviors of people throughout the world!

The awesome possibilities of mind control raise some very basic moral and ethical questions: Does anyone have the right to direct the thinking and behavior of others? Can there be any justification for robbing individuals of the freedom to think and believe what they want? Is mind control acceptable if its goals are generally considered good by society? Should self-administered forms of mind control be allowed, as long as they harm no one?

There are no simple answers to these difficult questions. Yet the issue of mind control needs to be confronted. This book examines eight prevalent types of mind control. As you read the various sections, you will acquire information and gain insights into this fascinating subject. It is hoped that an improved understanding will make you better able to take sides on the increasingly important issue of mind control.

CHAPTER 2.

CULT CONVERSION

Cult Conversion: The act of successfully
pressuring an individual to join any of several
religious groups that reject many of society's
values and demand unquestioning obedience
on the part of members; the process of an
individual's personality changing in response to
such pressure.

ALICE'S STORY

In her teen years, Alice was a successful, attractive,
independent young woman. She got along well with
her parents, protested war and injustice, and sup-
ported efforts to protect the environment. In her
spare time, Alice took nature photographs, wrote po-
etry, read, painted, and enjoyed the outdoors. When
she was eighteen, she entered college in Texas.

On her way to the library one morning, Alice passed
three young people collecting signatures on a petition
protesting the slaughter of whales. Alice stopped off
and added her name to their list. At the same time, she

began to chat with one of the young people, a clean-cut, handsome young man, who seemed very warm and friendly. At lunch, she found that he and his two friends shared many of her interests, including her concerns about pollution of the air and water. She cut the rest of her classes just to be with them. By evening, they invited her to spend a weekend at the farm commune where they lived. Alice agreed right away.

On Alice's visit to the farm, the group members overwhelmed her with friendship, warmth, love, and kindness. (This is called "love bombing.") Everyone seemed very idealistic. They said they wanted peace and an end to poverty and hunger in the world. It made Alice feel good just to hear them speak.

A few months later, Alice returned to the farm for a longer visit. She was given a full schedule of activities that kept her occupied for about eighteen hours a day. Constant prayers, meditation, lectures, discussions, songs, and even children's games filled every minute of her waking hours. Alice had little time to question the purposes of the group. With only a few hours of sleep a night, she also felt slightly groggy and unable to think clearly.

Another curious aspect of life on the farm that Alice could not help noticing was that she was never left alone. Having a group member with her at all times—even when she went to the bathroom—prevented her from comparing reactions with others visiting for the first time. It also kept her from telephoning her friends or family, or even from writing letters.

Nevertheless, Alice did enjoy being part of the group. She felt good when the group showered her with praise for taking part in their activities. It pleased her to be urged to join them on a permanent basis. They said they would take care of all her needs, and ask nothing in return, if she became a member. When the time came to decide, Alice didn't hesitate. She accepted eagerly.

In short order, Alice dropped out of college, broke most of the ties to her family, attempted to sign over her savings, and put her every thought and action at the service of the group.

Dr. John G. Clark, Jr., a professor of psychiatry at Harvard University Medical School, has studied people like Alice who join cults. He has even given this kind of changeover a name. He calls it cult conversion.

WHAT ARE CULTS?

After she joined, Alice discovered that the farm group was really part of the Unification Church, under the world-wide leadership of Reverend Sun Myung Moon. Its members are commonly known as Moonies. Most people consider the Unification Church a cult. Exact definitions of cults are hard to come by. But the Inter-faith Coalition of Concern About Cults says that cults have three basic characteristics:

1. A self-appointed leader who is worshiped by group members. The leader claims to have divine powers and exercises complete control over every aspect of the members' lives.

2. The use of mind-control techniques to direct the thoughts and beliefs of the members. These methods often lead to significant personality changes in the people within the cult.

3. The practice of lies and deceptions. Dishonest means may be employed to recruit and hold members, and to raise funds—the major activity of most cults.

According to Dr. Margaret T. Singer, an expert on cults, there are now about two thousand such groups in this country, with a membership of perhaps three million. In addition to the Unification Church, other large groups that are often classified as cults include the Children of God, the Hare Krishnas, the Divine Light Mission, and the Church of Scientology. Most members did not know they were joining a cult when they first came into these groups.

Various studies have produced a profile of the typical cult member: He or she is usually between eighteen and twenty-six years of age. Some 60 percent are male. About 93 percent are white. The vast majority come from middle- or upper-class homes. They are all average or above average in intelligence; over half have attended college.

At the time they join, most members can be described as "loners." They are people who do not easily form strong attachments to others. Often they come into the cult at a time of great personal crisis or transition in their lives—just after the death of a parent, entering or leaving college, breaking up a romance, making a career change, or moving into a new community. But perhaps the most common characteristic of prospective cult members is their idealism. These young people sincerely want to achieve a more meaningful existence for themselves and a better life for all.

METHODS AND TECHNIQUES

Almost all cults base their principles on those of the established religions. But their particular practices usually differ very considerably from all the traditional religious bodies. The stated purpose of most cults is to fight evil, sin, and corruption. To accomplish this goal they raise large amounts of money. In his testimony before the California Senate Select

Committee on Children and Youth in August 1974, Ted Patrick, an active opponent of cults, said, "Right in San Diego, I can account for over $2 billion; in Los Angeles I can account for almost a billion dollars. . . ." Yet most of these huge sums stay within the group.

Exact figures on money controlled by the cults is not known, but the daily newspapers have reported the following examples: the Unification Church has assets of over $15 million (*The New York Times*, April 19, 1982); the Bhagwan Shree Rajneesh owns two dozen Rolls-Royce automobiles and bought a $6-million Oregon ranch in 1981 (*The New York Times*, September 24, 1981 and December 19, 1982); and the dissolution of the People's Temple left $9.5 million in its treasury (*The New York Times*, February 26, 1983).

In many cults the members are led to believe that world disaster is imminent. They are taught that each individual is in danger of losing his or her soul to eternal damnation. Only the cult and its leader can save the members and the world from Satan and the forces of evil.

Cults usually expect members to obey orders and devote themselves exclusively to the group. Ties to family and friends outside the organization are discouraged, if not forbidden. Pressure to conform is aided by providing members with only limited and one-sided information. Any evidence that does not fit the basic beliefs or goals of the group is ignored.

Educational advancement and the furthering of personal objectives are usually not permitted; the primary study is of the group's dogma. Members are denied all but the most urgent medical and dental care. Private property is usually taken away in order to advance the group's goals and purposes.

Once Alice was part of the cult, she was assigned to a church group in Dallas. She raised money by selling flowers in the street. Every day Alice was awakened at 5:00 A.M. for prayers and chanting, followed by clean-up chores and breakfast. By 7:00 A.M. she was on the street for the whole day, lugging heavy cartons of flowers and running, not walking, to sell her quota. After a dinner break at the house, she had to attend a lecture and study. At 10:00 P.M. she was out on the street again to sell more flowers. Three hours later, she was finally allowed to return and go to sleep.

Alice and the other members were so strongly committed to the group that they would do anything to advance their cause. When they were trying to raise money in a Jewish neighborhood, for example, they would say that the money was going to help Jews. On college campuses, they claimed that the money was being put into a scholarship fund for needy students.

Deceptive practices are so common in cults that they have been given names. Members of the Unification Church call them Heavenly Deception. Among the Hare Krishnas, they are known as Transcendental Trickery. This refusal to deal honestly with the outside world is believed to stem from the belief that all nonmembers are part of the world of Satan. Since outsiders are evil enemies, they may be duped with impunity.

In Alice's church house, the doctrines of the group were repeated constantly. All new members were expected to study the cult's views and theories. Alice was taught that her life before joining was evil and sinful. She was made to feel guilty for what she had done in the past. Without the love of her parents and the support of friends, Alice came to depend entirely on the cult members for her personal satisfaction.

The food served at mealtimes was usually inadequate. Not only was the quality poor and limited in amount, but the diet was seldom very nutritious. An extreme example is described in Min S. Yee and Thomas N. Layton's book, *In My Father's House.* The basic daily diet in Jonestown, the Guyana center of the People's Temple, consisted of a breakfast of "rice and gravy or biscuits and syrup," a lunch of "a couple of pieces of bread and a bowl of watery rice soup," and "more rice, with beans" for dinner. Chicken was served once a month, an egg each Sunday and vegetables two or three times a week.

While members never starved, the effect of such low-protein, high-carbohydrate diets is a distinct lack of energy and an impaired ability to reason.

Cult services and prayer meetings are also specially designed to keep people in the group. Most require the members to shout and sing the prayers—the louder the better. They are urged to dance and do the other physical movements, such as bowing and kneeling, with great spirit and energy. Often, the extreme rapidity of breathing brings on a state of hyperventilation. Members feel light-headed and dizzy, and of course find it difficult to concentrate.

Other services strive to achieve an almost hypnotic effect. These sessions are conducted in dimly lit rooms filled with the smell of incense and soundproofed against outside noises. Many prayers, which may last hours at a time, are conducted in soft monotones and with much repetition. Some chants are uttered again and again, without change. The droning of the voices and the lack of any stimulation lends a spiritual, otherworldly quality to the proceedings.

Sometimes the cult members are forced to submit to cruel and humiliating punishments. In *Six Years with God*, Jeannie and Al Mills tell how Linda, their sixteen-year-old daughter, was punished by Reverend Jim Jones, the one-time leader of the People's Temple.

Linda was reportedly seen hugging another girl who had left the People's Temple. For this "evil" act, she was called up at a church service and forced to confess to the offense. Jim Jones ordered a spanking of seventy-five strokes with a heavy wooden paddle. Two guards grabbed Linda's wrists and ankles and held her suspended in the air, facedown, while a strong woman administered the beating.

After the girl received the punishment, according to the Mills' account, a guard handed the sobbing girl a microphone. Barely able to speak, she gasped out, "Thank you, Father," before being helped out of the room. Linda's faith in the church was so strong that she later said she deserved the beating. She looked on it as proof that Jim Jones really loved and cared about her.

PERSONALITY CHANGES

Alice's cult experience brought about shocking changes in her personality. The most obvious was her complete acceptance of everything she was told without question. She no longer had her own very special thoughts, hopes, and desires. Her value system and goals became identical to those of all the others in the cult, and were in complete agreement with the leader's ideas.

Her parents noted several psychological characteristics in Alice that are frequently found in cult members. Emotionally, she seemed dull and blunted. She showed neither joy nor sadness, happiness nor remorse, love nor hate. She seldom laughed, no matter how funny the situation. And she rarely became angry, despite the most vexing circumstances.

When talking about the group, she was very defensive and thought along narrow, inflexible lines. She showed no concern for her own needs or desires, and cared little about others. Before she could make any decision, she needed to consult with cult leaders. Her attention span was very short, and she found it almost impossible to deal with complex problems.

BREAKING FREE

Some cult members rise in the ranks and remain in these groups forever, although gray-haired individuals are very rare. Some manage to leave on their own, but this is very difficult to do. Still others are helped to get out of the cult and back to normal life through a process known as deprogramming.

Deprogramming is an attempt to rid members of the effects of cult conversion. It helps them readjust to living outside the cult and taking charge of their own lives.

Ted Patrick is one of the best-known deprogrammers. He has been successful with about 1,600 cult members; 30 later returned. Galen Kelly, another deprogrammer, brought out a total of 130 young people; 12 went back. The deprogramming usually works best with people who have spent less than one year in the cult. Longtime members find it much more difficult to change set ways of thinking and acting.

Alice, for instance, was deprogrammed after nearly four years in the Unification Church. Her father started the process by getting in touch with an organization in Tucson, Arizona, which helps parents get their children out of cults. The foundation has a four-part program to accomplish this purpose.

The first step is for the parents to be appointed the legal guardians of their children, even though they are over the age of eighteen. To do this, the parents must go to court and convince the judge that their children are being held in a group by mental or physical pressure.

The second step is for the parents, on their own, to locate the child and remove him or her from the cult. Sometimes the cult member agrees to leave willingly. Other times, the parents may resort to forcible kidnapping.

Once the individual is away from the influence of the group, the deprogrammer is ready for the third step. Someone, usually a former cult member, talks to the person over a period of several days. The young man or woman is given a clear idea of what has been happening. The deprogrammer describes and explains the methods that have been used to get recruits into the cult and keep them there. And the cult member is helped to understand the group's real purposes and objectives.

If the deprogramming is successful, the member decides to leave the group forever. The usual fourth step, then, is a month or more of psychological and physical rehabilitation at a center set up for this purpose.

In Alice's case, she consented to go to the deprogrammer, even though she had no thought of leaving the church. An ex-Moonie became her counselor. For nearly two weeks, he discussed the activities of the church with her. He pointed out the methods that had been used to attract her to the group, and the techniques that had kept her there. He asked basic questions about the church that she was unable to answer: Why is the sole occupation of the church to raise money? What happens to all the money that members bring in? Is the money ever used to help members or people outside the group?

At first, Alice resisted the deprogramming. Slowly, though, she began to wonder about the real purposes of the church. Her conflicts and confusion grew as she struggled to understand the entire experience.

Finally she came to realize that she had been the victim of a skillful cult conversion. She began to see that the chief role of the church was to increase its own wealth and power. At last, Alice made up her mind to leave the Unification Church.

Some experts believe that cult membership peaked in the 1970s, and that they are now losing members. Others say that, having become rich and powerful, the cults are here to stay. Almost everyone agrees, however, that cults will exist as long as people are attracted by their idealistic claims and can be manipulated by the techniques of cult conversion.

WATERLOO HIGH SCHOOL LIBRARY
1464 INDUSTRY RD.
ATWATER, OHIO 44201

CHAPTER 3.

BRAINWASHING

Brainwashing: A method of changing beliefs or
attitudes by the application of powerful
psychological pressure.

The word "brainwashing" was first made popular in
the United States by writer Edward Hunter in three
books that he wrote between 1951 and 1965. According to Hunter, the word was first used by the Chinese
around the year 1949. It probably sprang from an
ancient Buddhist expression, "heart washing." This
refers to an older man's going off by himself to meditate for a period of time while his children take care
of his worldly affairs.

BACKGROUND

The actual practice of brainwashing dates back to the
Middle Ages and the days of the Inquisition. During

that time, the Roman Catholic Church sought to find and punish all those who did not accept the teachings of the Church. Many nonbelievers were forced to convert to Christianity. The methods of the Inquisition included intense questioning, humiliation of suspects, and of course, the use of torture and threats of death for the recalcitrant.

Over the centuries since then, brainwashing has often been used to control and alter people's religious and political convictions. In recent history, there were the so-called Moscow purge trials of the 1930s. Scores of leading Soviet citizens confessed to dreadful crimes against the state. Most of their confessions, it is believed, went far beyond any actual crimes they may have committed.

The prisoners were subjected to ceaseless questioning to obtain these confessions. They were kept in isolation, their sleep was disturbed, and they were fed an unhealthy and sparse diet. The guards abused and humbled them, and forced them to live in unsanitary conditions. The only contact the prisoners had with the outside world was through their captors. The result was a weakening of the will of the prisoners. Once their will was broken, they were ready to follow the dictates of their captors.

The Chinese learned their mind-control methods

from the Russians. After the 1949 Communist revolution in China, they used these ways to gain control over those Chinese who did not accept the new system. Westerners who were suspected of working against the Communist state were also arrested and subjected to this kind of pressure.

Dr. Robert Jay Lifton, professor of psychiatry at Yale University, studied the techniques used by the Chinese Communists during the early 1950s. According to Dr. Lifton, the process began by establishing complete physical control over the prisoners. This made them feel passive and helpless.

Suspects were often questioned at unexpected times and for uncertain lengths of time. Their words were distorted; the meanings of their sentences were altered. They were looked on as representatives of all that was evil and sinful. Many grew increasingly confused and anxious. It became difficult for them to distinguish the truth from lies.

As the pressure built, many prisoners gave in. It was the only way they could find to avoid a complete mental breakdown. Accepting the new doctrine would save them from the relentless pressure. Perhaps it would help them regain some kindness and respect. They came to accept the belief system of their captors.

THE NORTH KOREAN EXPERIENCE

The most widespread use of brainwashing came during the Korean War (1950–1953), when the United States fought to protect South Korea from an invasion by Communist North Korea. The North Koreans used brainwashing methods that they had learned from the Chinese on the American prisoners of war (POWs). A number of these men ended up confessing to horrible atrocities that they committed against the Korean people—even though there was no truth in what they said.

In one incident, in 1951, a flier from the United States Air Force, captured by the North Koreans, was brought into a room to talk to reporters from North Korea and Communist China. He had been a POW since his plane was shot down a year earlier.

The prisoner first begged forgiveness for himself and other Americans for the sins they had committed against the Korean people. He told of being ordered to bomb North Korean schools and hospitals. It is also true, he said, that America was practicing germ warfare in North Korea. He himself had dropped containers filled with deadly germs over several big cities in North Korea. While praising the life and value system in Korea, he condemned American society. In conclusion, he said he hoped only to be allowed to remain in Korea and become part of their wonderful society.

The confession was prominently featured in newspapers of the Communist world. As copies reached the United States, government officials denied ever bombing civilians or using germ warfare in Korea. They said the pilot had been brainwashed. The process had led this patriotic aviator to confess to crimes that were never committed.

Dr. Louis Jolyon West, a psychiatrist who studied American POWs after the Korean War, summed up the North Koreans' method of brainwashing as Debility, Dependency, and Dread (DDD).

First, the victims were imprisoned and deprived of an adequate diet. They were fed enough to stay alive, but little more. Seldom were they allowed to sleep through an entire night without interruption. As a result, they were always a little tired and very weak. This made them less alert and unable to resist the will of others.

Although instances of violence were rare, there were frequent warnings of torture and even death. The usual pattern was to threaten the prisoner, and then, at the very last moment, to issue a reprieve. The POWs were continually accused of wrongdoing and humiliated for supposed crimes. They were barraged with Communist ideas and given no opportunity to argue or defend themselves.

The prisoners were forced to turn to their captors for everything necessary for life—even for permission to go to the bathroom. This made them increasingly dependent. Since they were so far from family and friends, the POWs felt completely alienated. The absence of newspapers, a radio, or other sources of stimulation further dulled the mind and spirit.

Any personal contact with the captors came to be appreciated. A smile, a kind word, or any small favor was received with gratitude. The fact that the guards were friendly from time to time made the prisoners especially eager to please them. The prisoners began to regard their captors as sincere people. They sought their support and approval.

Eventually, the inmates started to accept the enemy's ideas. They admitted many supposed misdeeds and pledged their devotion to the Communist cause. The officials encouraged this behavior by rewarding them when they showed signs of weakening, and punishing ideas and actions that they considered stubborn.

The POWs who returned to the United States were found to be considerably changed by the treatment they had endured in North Korean jails. Of the fifty-nine POWs studied by Dr. West, thirty-six had confessed to war crimes of various kinds. These men said they hated America, believed in Communism, and upheld the North Korean point of view. Many turned away from family and friends.

Dr. West and other researchers concluded that brainwashing had broken down the men's personalities. But other experts came to different conclusions. Of an estimated 3,500 American POWs that they studied, they found that fewer than 50, about one and one half percent, were successfully brainwashed by the North Koreans. At the end of the war in 1953, no more than 25 of them chose to remain in North Korea. And by the 1980s only 10 were left, two tenths of one percent. They compare these figures with the American Civil War, when as many as one percent of the captured soldiers switched and fought for the other side—and without brainwashing!

BRAINWASHING IN AMERICA

Not long ago a case of brainwashing in America caught the attention of the entire world. In this incident, brainwashing was not carried out by the government, but by an illegal group. And its target was not large numbers of people, but a single victim.

Patricia Hearst, twenty-year-old daughter of a millionaire family, was kidnapped on the evening of February 4, 1974. Members of a small underground revolutionary group, the Symbionese Liberation Army (SLA), captured Patty and took her to an apartment in San Francisco. She was bound, blindfolded, and locked in a closet. The only times she was allowed out were to go to the bathroom and for a once-a-week bath.

While she was confined in the closet, the SLA members grilled her daily. They asked endless questions about her father's fortune—how much he had, where he made it, and so on. They accused her family of crimes against the poor. "You're a prisoner of war," they said, "and you're going to be tried for their crimes." To add to the pressure, several times SLA members held loaded guns to her head and threatened to kill her. The others laughed at her fright and at her cries for mercy.

Patty was forced to tape-record messages asking for money to further the group's aims. When her parents did not comply with demands that they contribute $400 million worth of food to the nation's poor as a condition for her release, Patty was told that her parents no longer loved her or cared about her fate. At the same time, they inspired her with their idealistic talk of sharing the nation's wealth among the poor.

After nearly two months of being confined to a closet, Patty was given a choice. She could either join the group or be punished by death. When she chose to live, they allowed her out of the closet, but still watched her very closely. Most of her time was spent listening to lectures on the theories and ideals of the SLA. Also, she was given training on how to handle a gun.

On April 14, 1974, Patty and others in the SLA robbed a bank in San Francisco. Photographs taken by bank cameras show Patty aiming a gun at customers as other SLA members gathered up $10,000. The following month, when two SLA members were caught shoplifting, Patty sprayed the building with bullets to help their escape. On September 18, 1975, she was arrested and charged with taking part in both crimes.

Patty's lawyer offered the court the defense that the young woman had been brainwashed. It became the first case in history in which brainwashing was on trial. The two biggest brainwashing experts, Dr. Robert Jay Lifton and Dr. Louis Jolyon West, testified that this was a classic example of brainwashing. Patty had been made completely dependent on her captors. She had been isolated and deprived of outside contact other than with group members. Fearing for her life, she had begun to believe what her captors told her. Her participation in the robberies was an automatic reaction to her indoctrination.

The jury, though, was not convinced by these arguments. Patty Hearst was found guilty of the criminal acts, and was sentenced to a term in jail.

The verdict did little to settle the main questions of brainwashing: Do the techniques work? Can people really be brainwashed? Can human minds and actions be controlled by severe mental pressure? If brainwashing works, how long do its effects last? And finally, who is to be held responsible for the behavior of the so-called brainwashed—the victim or the oppressor?

CHAPTER 4.

MIND DRUGS

Mind Drugs: Chemical substances that affect the human brain in significant ways.

Most Americans get the message from our society that it is perfectly acceptable to "take something" to make yourself feel better. Thus, many people use dozens of different kinds of pills and other substances to eliminate pain, bring on sleep, fight fatigue, calm jittery nerves, cheer up, relax, or simply "turn on." These chemicals, which work by affecting some part of the brain, are called mind drugs. They are also known as psychoactive or neuroleptic substances.

The exact effect of the mind drugs on the brain is still not fully known. But there is no doubt that certain changes do take place. And few doubt that mind drugs have become an important way of practicing mind control on others or on oneself.

MINOR TRANQUILIZERS

Minor tranquilizers are drugs that are used to reduce anxiety and tension in people who are troubled, but are not suffering from mental illness. An estimated two million Americans, or about one out of every ten adults, take a minor tranquilizer regularly. People of both sexes, all ages, and on every social and economic level take minor tranquilizers. The figures, though, show that twice as many women as men are given these substances. Valium, Librium, and Miltown are the most frequently prescribed minor tranquilizers. Around one hundred million prescriptions for Valium alone are written every year.

Several patients in one study were asked to describe their experiences with tranquilizers. In general, those taking the drugs said they felt more comfortable and less frightened. But they also cared less about their day-to-day activities, and felt more helpless about their futures. Off drugs, most had more anxiety, sleeplessness, and feelings of panic. There was, however, a sense of being in control of their fates and a stronger motivation to improve. Overall, the use of minor tranquilizers seems sometimes to lessen the symptoms of mental distress. But it rarely solves the basic problem.

ANTIPSYCHOTIC DRUGS

Antipsychotic drugs date from the early 1950s, when they first came into widespread use for the treatment of serious mental disorders known as psychoses. With these drugs, doctors became able to control many of the symptoms of psychoses, such as extreme agitation, wide swings of mood, and deep depression. Patients are generally able to function better while taking the drugs. Many who required hospital care or confinement now take drugs which enable them to live with their families and work at jobs in the community.

Some of the most widely used antipsychotic drugs are the so-called major tranquilizers. The most popular have the trade names Thorazine, Haldol, Mellaril, and Stelazine. These substances are often prescribed for patients suffering with schizophrenia, a severe disorder that may include bizarre behavior, delusions, hallucinations, and withdrawal into a fantasy world. The drugs can often control the violent behavior and quiet the wild delusions and hallucinations in patients with this disorder. They can also bring some patients out of a state of withdrawal.

Sinequan, Tofranil, and Elavil are common anti-depressants, or energizers. They are used to treat severe depression, a condition characterized by general apathy, and little or no interest in others or in one's surroundings. When depressed patients are given these drugs, they often become much more active and involved in the life around them.

Lithium salts, such as lithium carbonate, are called antimanics. They are very effective in treating the wild mood swings of people with manic-depressive psychosis. Patients with this condition tend to alternate between periods of depression and periods of agitation and excitement. The drug calms most patients during the manic episodes, and energizes them when they are depressed. It also helps to lessen the violent swings from one extreme to the other.

Some studies on the effects of antipsychotic drugs are quite impressive. Forty percent fewer women with schizophrenia who were treated with a major tranquilizer suffered a relapse than those who did not receive such a drug. Another survey showed that 60 to 70 percent of people previously hospitalized with schizophrenia who did not receive major tranquilizers were back in institutions within a year. The rate for those who received one of the drugs was 10 to 15 percent lower.

Not all reports on antipsychotic drugs, however,

are this favorable. A number of side effects may accompany their use.

Patients under treatment often are indifferent or apathetic, feel continuously drowsy, or have difficulty using their hands, walking, talking, reading, and concentrating. Prolonged use can cause permanent brain damage, resulting in a disfiguring and disabling condition known as tardive dyskinesia. Such patients show slurred speech and involuntary twitching of the lips, tongue, and facial muscles. Although there are some ways to help people with tardive dyskinesia, there is no known cure.

HALLUCINOGENS

There is a large number of mind drugs that people take themselves, without prescription and without consulting a doctor. They are known as illicit drugs, since they are usually bought and sold illegally.

The hallucinogens make up one group of illicit drugs. They work on the brain and nervous system to bring about changes in the user's feelings, thoughts, sensations, and perceptions. LSD (lysergic acid diethylamide), PCP (phencyclidine), and mescaline are the most commonly used hallucinogens. They are also known as psychedelics, a word created in 1956 that literally means "revealing to the mind." The term has come to refer, though, to the sensations caused by the hallucinogens.

People under the influence of hallucinogens often experience strong feelings of well-being or euphoria, which may reach a state of ecstasy. These powerful emotions are sometimes accompanied by quick swings from great joy to deep sorrow.

Perhaps the most striking effect of hallucinogens, though, is that experiences become much more intense. Sounds become louder and richer; colors appear brighter; smells and tastes are stronger. Sometimes the senses cross over, and users "hear" the color purple or "see" the smell of a rose. Floors and walls seem to sway. The dimensions of time and space either stretch out or shrink. And finally, there may be hallucinations—sights and sounds that do not exist in reality, but that are very real to the person taking the drug.

Reactions to hallucinogens, more than any other drug, depend on what the users expect to happen, and where, when, and with whom the drug is taken. Also, the effects are usually stronger for adolescents than for adults.

Some of the most acute responses to hallucinogens include mental confusion and paranoia. Many users feel themselves losing control and fear that they are going insane. Negative emotions, depression, and feelings of helplessness may overwhelm them. Particularly dangerous, however, is the belief users sometimes get that they are all-powerful and incapable of being hurt. People on hallucinogens have been known to jump out of windows and walk in front of speeding cars, often with fatal results.

Powerful reactions to the drugs, called flashbacks, can occur suddenly and without warning during a drug-free period, even years later. Flashbacks can last from a few minutes up to several hours. Since they may occur at any time, they can lead to serious accidents. Long-term reactions include prolonged anxiety, depression, and mental disturbance. Serious mental illness may strike individuals who are already troubled.

NARCOTICS

People who use narcotics, it is believed, take the substances to bring about a sense of euphoria and overall mental well-being that makes worries and problems seem much less important. Narcotics, also called opiates, cloud the mind, reduce the ability to feel pain, and make the user feel drowsy. The most familiar narcotics are heroin, morphine, and opium, which are natural products, and methadone, which is a synthetic opiate.

Scientists are able to trace the movement of narcotics within the body. They find that there are spots on the nerve cells, or neurons, within the brain to which the molecules of the narcotic substances become attached. These spots are called opiate receptors. The molecules then enter the neurons, and bring about the mental changes associated with narcotics.

Narcotics are addictive. That is, regular users develop a powerful physical and psychological need and craving for the substance. The addicts are so strongly drawn to continue use of the drug that they will risk jail, the loss of a job, the breakup of a family, or permanently ruined health to maintain the drug habit.

When users give up the narcotics, they suffer a period of withdrawal. The first symptoms include irritability, tremors, chills and sweating, vomiting, runny eyes and nose, muscle aches, abdominal pains, and diarrhea. After about forty-eight hours, the withdrawal symptoms reach a peak. There are also pains in the back, arm, and leg muscles, which lead to kicking movements. This may explain the origin of the expression "kicking the habit." In about one week, the withdrawal symptoms begin to fade and disappear.

ALCOHOL AND MARIJUANA

Like other drugs, alcohol affects the mind of the user. Drinks, such as whiskey, rum, brandy, gin, vodka, wine, and beer, contain various percentages of alcohol. When someone takes one of these drinks, the alcohol enters the bloodstream and some gets carried to the brain. Here it lowers the level of activity of certain brain cells. It particularly weakens the parts of the brain that control behavior.

The first drink usually releases inhibitions and makes drinkers feel more relaxed. Those who have two and a half drinks within an hour find that the alcohol affects their judgment. Drinkers do and say things they would not do or say without the alcohol.

The blood-alcohol level reaches 0.10 percent after about five shots of whiskey or the same number of cans of beer in an hour. This amount of alcohol affects the parts of the brain that control the muscles of the body. Speech becomes slurred. Physical movements are sloppy and not well coordinated. Reaction time is slower than usual.

Each additional drink disrupts more functions of the brain. Emotions become erratic. The intoxicated person may change from laughter to tears in just moments. Judgment, coordination, and perception are badly affected. The person may pass out. Twelve drinks within a short time can paralyze the part of the brain responsible for breathing, and the drinker may go into a coma and die.

Many people who smoke marijuana, which is also

called pot or grass, compare it to drinking a little alcohol. They say it gives them the same high, the same good, relaxed feeling. A few feel that marijuana helps them do difficult tasks better and more easily. Others say it helps them to forget their problems.

Different people, though, react in different ways to marijuana. Some become active, and speak more than usual. Others grow quiet and withdrawn. Those who expect to have a pleasant high usually have a good reaction. People who are afraid may become ill, or even develop "pot panic," which is a fear that they are going insane.

Normally, marijuana does not cause mental problems. But people who are having emotional difficulties often find their condition is made worse with marijuana. There is some evidence, too, that longtime, regular users of marijuana may show some permanent ill effects from the drug. For some, reaction time slows down, and they may lose some motor control. It becomes hard for them to learn anything new, and their attention tends to wander. Also, they may forget things they know perfectly well, and find that time and space seem to be changing.

SEDATIVES AND STIMULANTS

In small doses, sedatives relieve anxiety and tension; in larger doses, they put people to sleep. Most of the sedatives are barbiturates, which are various compounds of a substance known as barbital. Among the fifteen in use today, the best known are Nembutal, Seconal, and Amytal.

Barbiturates are particularly active in the cortex, or "thinking" part of the brain. Their chief effects, similar to alcohol intoxication, are felt about a half hour after use and last for up to six hours.

Doctors prescribe barbiturates to calm and soothe patients, or as sleeping pills to treat insomnia. Nonmedical abusers use these substances to control their thoughts and induce a general sense of well-being.

Regular, repeated use of high levels of barbiturates can lead to dependency or addiction. Stopping usage suddenly leads to serious, painful symptoms. Some heavy users go into convulsions, hallucinate, and become delirious.

A barbiturate overdose is a real danger. A slight overdose makes the person look and act drunk; a heavy overdose results in a weak and rapid pulse as well as difficulty in breathing. In extreme cases it can lead to death.

Stimulants have the opposite effect on users. They are supposed to make people feel stronger and more alert. They lessen feelings of fatigue or tiredness, and create a sensation of euphoria. Among the stimulants, cocaine and the amphetamines are the most widely known and used.

Cocaine is a powerful substance that acts directly on the brain. It makes the heart beat faster and causes the blood pressure to rise. People on cocaine are often very talkative and show little interest in eating.

When the cocaine is sniffed through the nose or injected, users get a sudden and intense feeling of pleasure. After only a short time, though, the euphoria is followed by a deep depression and a need for more of the substance. Irritability, anxiety, and some mental confusion follow a mild overdose. Longtime addiction leads to depression, often with irrational fears that people and things are out to harm the cocaine user.

Amphetamines give users the same sort of euphoria as is reported from cocaine, though the effect is not as powerful. The heavy use of amphetamines may give rise to addiction. Regular users, when deprived of the drug, crave another dose. With withdrawal come depression, cramps, sleepiness, apathy, irritability, and mental confusion.

BENEFITS AND RISKS

The use of drugs to control behavior is not new to this century. But certainly the extent of use and the numbers of people who are dependent on them is greater than ever before. That is why it is so important to stay informed about all mind drugs, legal and illicit.

The antipsychotic drugs, now the main method of treating severe mental illness, have recently come under attack by some psychiatrists, mental patients, and others. Despite their benefits, many now say that the purpose of the drugs is to control and stupefy people with mental disorders, not to treat them. They claim that the drugs are like "knockout" pills. They blunt thinking, and destroy initiative and creativity. While the drugs may relieve many of the symptoms of mental illness, there is evidence that prolonged use results in conditions that may be as bad as those that the drugs were meant to improve.

Many forms of drug use create the possibility of addiction. As people get accustomed to certain substances, they become more and more psychologically and physically dependent on them. Continued use may result in distorted thinking or mental confusion.

The use of illicit drugs often provides pleasure and relief from stress, and improves the state of mind. But at the same time there are disturbing side effects. Before taking *any* drug that affects the way you think and act, it is wise to carefully consider both the benefits and the risks.

CHAPTER 5.

ALTERED STATES

Altered State: Any conscious mental state that is different from an individual's normal, alert, awake state.

You have probably experienced an altered state more than once in your life. Perhaps it occurred while you were daydreaming during a long walk or a ride in a car, bus, or plane. Your mind may have wandered while listening to an especially dull speaker. If you are like many people, you may enter an altered state just before falling asleep, or as you wake up. Altered states often occur while dancing vigorously or being hurled around at great speed on an amusement park ride. Sometimes a very emotional religious observance can bring about such mind changes.

WHAT IS AN ALTERED STATE?

During an altered state, you cannot control your thinking. You lose all sense of where you are. The way you feel resembles dreaming—except that you aren't asleep. Unrelated images and ideas flash through your mind. Your thoughts do not move along in their usual logical, step-by-step way. Instead they jump about without apparent sense or connection. All of your attention focuses on these strange visions or thoughts.

Many people have described their experiences in altered states. The reports, of course, vary from person to person. But almost all say that the sensations are very real and vivid. And most regard altered states as highly valued life occurrences.

Sigmund Freud wrote of three levels of consciousness—conscious, preconscious, and subconscious. The conscious level is our normal, alert, awake state. The preconscious level holds memories that are easily brought to the conscious mind. The subconscious also holds memories, but these are more difficult to bring to the conscious level. (Freudian psychoanalysis tries to bring memories from the subconscious into the conscious level, thereby helping to rid individuals of problems caused by their repression.)

Following this three-level scheme of consciousness,

the altered state is a fourth level, the level above the conscious. It is super-consciousness. Other terms that have been used to describe the altered state are cosmic consciousness, mystical state, peak experience, *satori*, *samadhi*, ecstasy, and oceanic unity. One expert collected a list of twenty-four such names. Each has a slightly different meaning. But all describe the capacity of the mind to function on another, higher level. And this level is recognized, either by the individual or by an observer, as different from the normal state of consciousness.

In an altered state, the individual's perceptions can change greatly. Five minutes may seem to last an hour or more, or flash by in what feels like a few seconds. The person may feel able to cover a distance of hundreds of miles with just one step. Colors, sounds, tastes, and odors all become much brighter and more attractive.

Many people also report feeling changes in their bodies. Some are convinced they are growing to be ten or twenty feet tall. Others say they feel the size of a tiny doll. One high school student reported the sensation of his head seeming to become larger than the rest of his body. One woman said that her hands seemed to be glowing with a soft light. A man thought his body was covered with animal-like fur.

Along with such perceptual changes may come new

philosophical insights. One poet reports that he gets new understandings of life's purpose and the reason for his existence when in an altered state. His sense of self-importance diminishes, he says, as he glimpses the underlying forces that control the universe. Large numbers of people find that the altered state releases strong, positive feelings of joy, love, happiness, and contentment. It brings a surge of vigor and vitality to their lives, while helping to free them from stress and anxiety. Almost always, the experience is so positive that individuals try to achieve it again and again.

Most changes in the altered state are temporary. They may last for only a few minutes or hours at a time. But certain changes, such as a new viewpoint on life, may last forever.

MENTAL DISCIPLINE

Basically, one can enter an altered state in two ways—either through mental discipline or through body discipline. Yoga, Zen, and transcendental meditation are three well-known mental disciplines that can help a person enter an altered state of consciousness.

Yoga is a school of Hindu philosophy. The word comes from the Sanskrit and means union. More exactly, it refers to the mystical union between the self and the supreme being. The root of the word is the same as yoke, a device that joins animals together to perform a particular task.

To achieve the union, yogis (people who practice yoga) do a number of exercises. Some involve narrowing the field of concentration. That is, they try to focus on one object, word, or thought, to the exclusion of all else. Certain practices, called *pranayamas*, are designed to control breathing. This raises the level of carbon dioxide in the blood, bringing about certain desired changes in the mind. Then there are postures, or *asanas*, that the yogi holds. Usually awkward or difficult positions, they frequently contribute to the mystical experience.

Zen is considered a branch of Buddhism. But it is also a method used to achieve greater awareness of the self. One important Zen practice is wall gazing, or *zazen*. The idea is to clear one's mind and suspend thinking by concentrating on nothingness, on a blank wall. Correct breathing and posture help the individual achieve the altered state. Also vital to Zen is the *koan*, a type of conversation between the Zen master and the student. The purpose of the koan is to go beyond reason and logic in order to achieve enlightenment. For example, the master might ask, "What was your face like before you were born?" or "What is the sound of one hand clapping?" As the student tries to answer these questions—which really don't have answers—he or she discovers new and higher levels of consciousness.

The first raised stage of consciousness in Zen is called *satori*. It is a deeper awareness of reality and spirituality. With satori come feelings of power, of calmness and of great, controlled energy.

Even higher is the second stage, called *samadhi*. In this more trancelike state, the individual loses awareness of self and surroundings. The experience is so unlike ordinary consciousness that those who have entered samadhi have difficulty describing it to others. One famous experiment involved a Zen master who had achieved samadhi. Researchers plunged his hand into a bucket of ice water and kept it there for nearly one hour. The master gave no sign of pain or discomfort.

Meditation is a very old way of achieving an altered state by controlling the mind. It is an important part of both yoga and Zen, as well as many of the world's religions. Meditation relaxes the mind and frees it from conscious thoughts.

One popular form of meditation today is known as transcendental meditation, or TM. The TM procedure is simpler than yoga or Zen. In TM, the person sits in a comfortable chair, closes his or her eyes, and silently chants a mantra again and again. A mantra is a secret word given to the person by a TM master. By repeating and concentrating on the mantra, the person clears the mind of all other thoughts. The goal is to reach a state of pure consciousness, relaxed but alert.

BODY DISCIPLINE

Throughout history, fasting has been a way to enter an altered state. To fast means either to eat nothing or to severely limit the amounts or types of food eaten for a period of time.

Most religious observances include periods of fasting. Usually, the purpose of these fasts is to purify the body or to do penance for wrongdoings. Christians restrict the food that they eat during the forty days of Lent. The Jews observe a complete fast on Yom Kippur, the Day of Atonement. Faithful Moslems may neither eat nor drink from sunrise to sunset during the holy month of Ramadan.

Many Christians, in particular, experienced altered states as a result of their Lenten fasting during the Middle Ages. Food was often in short supply, especially in winter, when few plants grew and game was scarce. There were widespread nutritional deficiencies. Then, with the arrival of spring, came the fast of Lent. The combined effects of the food shortages of winter with the Lenten fast caused many to enter into altered states of consciousness.

But fasting, when carried on over a long period, weakens the body. The brain cells are damaged by the lack of vital protein, vitamins, and minerals. As a result, people may feel slightly faint and dizzy. They may lose their sense of time and place. Some see images and hear sounds that do not really exist.

Just as the body needs food each day, so it requires sleep. Most people are ready to go to sleep after being awake for fourteen to sixteen hours. If the sleepless period is extended to forty-eight hours, they become very tired. People who go even longer without sleep suffer some psychological changes. They become irritable, disorganized and disoriented. In one experiment, a radio disc jockey stayed awake for ten days. Toward the end of that time he was experiencing wild hallucinations and extreme distortions of reality. Many were attractive and pleasant; some, however, were very frightening.

Along with the daily requirements for food and sleep, humans need to breathe. From ancient times to today, certain people have mastered their breathing as a way of reaching an altered state. In almost all instances, the approach is to train the normal rate of breathing to slow down considerably.

As you know, normal breathing brings a continuous supply of oxygen into the lungs. From there the oxygen is carried by the blood to the body and brain cells. When breathing is slowed, the amount of oxygen is reduced. At the same time, a waste product given off by the body, carbon dioxide, builds up. The increased amount of carbon dioxide interferes with the function of the brain cells. Disorientation and hallucinations are the most frequent symptoms.

DANCE

Every society and culture, from the oldest to the most modern, has a dance tradition. Some of these dances have the effect of helping individuals to reach an altered state.

A passage in the Bible tells how King David "danced before the Lord with all his might." In ancient Greece the *maenads*, or mad women, performed wild, orgiastic dances dedicated to the god Dionysus. The priests in ancient Rome danced in a frenzied fashion, slashing and mutilating their bodies at the climax.

Entire towns and cities took part in hysterical dances during the Middle Ages. The mass dances ended only when all the dancers fell to the ground in trancelike states. A mystical order of Islam called the dervishes dates back to that time. Some are called whirling dervishes because they whirl around at great speeds during their worship, while repeating a special chant. Often this leads to mystical and religious visions.

The beating drums and rhythmic dancing of voodoo ceremonies bring the participants into a state of religious ecstasy. The national dance of Israel, the Hora, is a vigorous circle dance that excites those who take part and creates a rapturous group feeling. Some popular American social dances are done to loud, fast, repetitious music. They are often performed in hot, crowded rooms with flashing colored lights, and the mental effects can be most exhilarating.

Several factors are believed to account for the fact that fast, active, strenuous dances can change the participant's mental state. In going through the movements of the dances, the performers hyperventilate. Their breathing becomes very rapid and deep, leading to an increase in oxygen and a decrease in carbon dioxide in the body. This affects the brain cells and leads to changes in thinking and perceiving. Also, dances that involve much spinning and whirling may make people dizzy, causing mental confusion and loss of orientation. And finally, physically demanding dances that go on for long stretches of time may result in extreme fatigue, which can effect the mind's functioning.

SENSORY DEPRIVATION

Your five senses—touch, sight, hearing, taste, and smell—are always receiving impressions from the outside world. What happens when all or most of these impressions cease, when there is sensory deprivation? The result can be a change in consciousness.

Accounts from the past tell of many figures who practiced sensory deprivation, mostly to increase and deepen their religious experiences. Saint Anthony, for example, lived in the early years of the Christian era. As far as is known, he spent most of his life in silent solitude on a desert mountain in Egypt. One time he descended to organize a monastery and to encourage Christians to imitate his way of life. Then he returned to devote the rest of his life to his lonely vigil.

Hermits in the Himalayan Mountains of Tibet, among others, still follow the same practice of living in complete silence and isolation. From their writings, we learn that they undergo many mystical and visionary experiences. These happenings are believed to be due to their limited sensory input.

In 1954, while working at the National Institute of Mental Health in Bethesda, Maryland, Dr. John C. Lilly devised an experiment to test the limits of sensory deprivation. Dr. Lilly wanted to see what would happen to his mind with absolutely no stimulation from the outside.

Dr. Lilly immersed himself in a bathtublike water tank located in a room that was both soundproof and lightproof. The water in the tank was kept close to the body's skin temperature of ninety-three degrees. The researcher breathed through a face mask that had tubes extending above the surface of the water.

During the many hours he spent in the tank, Dr. Lilly passed through a number of dreamlike trances and mystical states. His descriptions matched those of the altered states of consciousness experienced by others.

ASCID

Jean Houston and Robert E. L. Masters are two researchers who have studied altered consciousness in their New York City laboratory. They use a simple apparatus called the ASCID, which is short for Altered States of Consciousness Induction Device. Essentially it is a metal swing that can move freely in any direction—back and forth, side to side, and around and around. The blindfolded subject stands on the swing platform, and is held in place by canvas bands. After a while, without any effort, unconscious movements of the subject's body set the ASCID into motion. The resulting dizziness and disorientation bring on the altered state.

Subjects on the ASCID enter into altered states in just a few minutes. One student of religion spent one and one half hours on the ASCID. He later reported a number of deeply moving, rapturous encounters with God. The experiences made him a better person, he said, and changed the quality of his life. Another subject told of going through several changes in his body image. He felt himself grow larger and then smaller, heavier and then lighter, disintegrated and then whole. Someone else said that she felt herself die and then come to life again.

WHIPPING AND FLOGGING

Among the most extreme ways of changing consciousness is assaulting the body. In ancient Egypt the devout were beaten as part of the worship of the god Isis. In ceremonies at the temple of Artemis Orthia at Sparta, Greece, children were thrashed until they bled. Women were whipped in the temple of Dionysus at Alea. The ancient Romans punished females by flogging during the annual Lupercalian festivals.

Punishing rituals continued in the early years of Christianity. In part, it was a penance for having sinned; in part, it was to achieve an ecstatic union with

God. Through the Middle Ages up to today, monasteries and fraternities of flagellants, as they are called, practice flogging. Often the whipping occurs in processions. Individuals walk through the streets bearing crosses, and beat on their own or each other's bare backs with leather thongs. Many pass into a mystical state during these observances. They frequently report seeing visions and receiving inspirational messages.

Flogging is thought to bring about mental changes in at least two ways. The pain and the excitement cause the body to release extra quantities of adrenalin and histamine, substances that are known to affect the way the brain works. Also, the flogging usually continues until the skin is broken. If standards of cleanliness are not too high, infections can result. When complications set in, the patients may become delirious, and in that way lose touch with reality.

Like some other forms of mind control, altered states of consciousness can be achieved by an individual or can be imposed on one person by others. For many, it is a glorious and unique mental experience. Some others find it frightening and unpleasant. But for everyone it is a fascinating subject to learn more about.

CHAPTER 6.

INSIGHT THERAPY

Insight Therapy: A way of solving psychological problems through talk between therapists and patients. By gaining an understanding of the root causes of difficulties, the patients can bring about improved patterns of behavior.

LINDA'S STORY

"I'm afraid!" Linda, a sixteen-year-old high school student, shouted. "I'm really, really scared! I never speak in class—even though I know the answer. I don't go to school socials—even though I love to dance. I don't try out for chorus—even though all my friends belong. I hate the way I act—but I just can't change."

While Linda sobbed loudly, Dr. Barnes waited a minute or two. Then she said, "Linda, I think I understand the pain you feel. Maybe I can help. Tell me, can you remember the first time you felt so terribly afraid?"

It took Linda a little while to pull herself together. Then she started recalling certain incidents from her childhood. She remembered how her older brother laughed at her when she mispronounced a word, or the way her father often ignored her when she spoke to him. Dr. Barnes gently interrupted from time to time to ask certain questions. She led the girl to talk about memories that Linda seemed to be pushing from her mind.

Linda had started seeing Dr. Barnes because she felt there was something wrong with her life, and she needed help to make it better. Dr. Barnes is a psychiatrist, a medical doctor who specializes in the treatment of mental disturbances and illnesses. Psychiatrists, along with psychologists and some types of social workers and counselors, are known as psychotherapists. They use mostly psychological techniques to help people solve their personal problems.

The type of psychotherapy that Dr. Barnes is using with Linda is known as insight therapy. There are many different types of insight therapy, but they all involve talk between patients and therapists. And they all aim to help the patients change thought processes or behavior patterns which, for one reason or another, are thought to be in need of improvement.

PSYCHOANALYSIS

Psychoanalysis is a very intense form of insight therapy that was originated around the beginning of the twentieth century by Sigmund Freud (1856–1939). In psychoanalysis, the patients are encouraged to talk freely about whatever enters their minds. The therapists, or analysts, interpret what is said. In this way, they help the patients arrive at an understanding of themselves and their problems.

In very simple terms, Freud held that people's behaviors are shaped by their inner or unconscious motives, attitudes, beliefs, and fears. If these unconscious drives are in conflict or are not accepted, the result is a disturbance in function—without any obvious cause. The goal of psychoanalysis, then, is to bring out the hidden feelings and unresolved conflicts, many dating back to childhood, that Freud considered the source of emotional difficulties. Once they are brought to the conscious level, the patient can deal with them.

Free association is one important tool of psychoanalysis. Patients are encouraged to relax, and to say whatever comes to mind as a way of revealing their unconscious thoughts. They are told to express all ideas, no matter how silly or unimportant they may seem.

Thus, a patient may start telling the therapist about a movie she saw, leave off to whistle a song, and suddenly remember the taste of her grandmother's cookies—all within a few minutes. Resting comfortably on a couch in a slightly darkened room, with the analyst out of the direct line of sight, the patients are able to focus all attention on expressing their innermost thoughts.

The analyst listens to the flow of ideas and tries to find clues, meanings, and interconnections that may not be obvious to the patient. Then the analyst may suggest certain possibilities that might underlie the subjects that come up by free association.

"What is the connection between the movie and the tune you whistled? Is it possible that you told me about your grandmother because it is too painful to talk about your mother?" Sometimes the therapist's questions or comments are based on things the patients say. Other times they are drawn from unspoken messages, which the therapist thinks might be repressed.

The therapist's job is to listen and try to interpret all the information the patient brings forth. But at the same time, the therapist knows that certain topics—childhood memories, strong emotions, recent dreams—usually have more significance than the price of gasoline or the status of teams in the world series, for example.

Dream interpretation serves the therapist as another valuable way to reach the patient's unconscious. Freud reasoned that one's defenses are more relaxed when one is asleep and dreaming. At those times, he believed, the unconscious was more easily accessible. In fact, Freud called dreams "the royal road to the unconscious." Analysts often ask patients to recount all their dreams, and together they try to interpret and analyze them.

After a time, some people in analysis begin unconsciously to transfer strong emotions that they once felt for parents or other important people in their lives to the analyst. A woman may fear and hate the analyst the way she was afraid of and angry at her father when she was a young girl. A man may feel jealous of his analyst just as he used to resent his older brother. This process, called transference, allows patients to reveal feelings to the analyst that may interfere with their relationships with others. Once brought to the surface, they can be examined. The patients can then learn to handle these feelings, and overcome the transference.

CLIENT-CENTERED THERAPY

Carl Rogers is a psychotherapist who developed a set of theories that are different from those of Freud. Rogers believed that the goal of therapy is to bring about a positive change in self-concept. Once people are satisfied with themselves, he said, they will interact much better with others. Reaching this goal involves the therapist's accepting the individual's emotions, thoughts, and values in a very loving and respectful way. In this nonthreatening atmosphere, the client (not called patient) moves toward self-fulfillment, or self-actualization.

In Rogers' client-centered approach, the therapist tries to see the world from the client's point of view, in a positive way, without passing judgment. Client-centered therapy does not focus on what happened in the past. Rather it deals with what the client is feeling and experiencing at the moment.

Ivan, thirty-seven years old, married with two young children, had an argument with his boss and quit his job at an electronics factory. He thought it would be easy to find another position, but after looking for nearly a month, he found nothing. Deeply depressed and upset, and filled with feelings of fear and guilt, he begins to see a client-centered therapist.

The therapist accepts and sympathizes with Ivan's

feelings. At the same time, the therapist tries to help him clarify his thoughts and emotions. In time, Ivan may relax and start to feel better about himself and what he did. With his new outlook, the analyst hopes Ivan will find a new job that is even better than the one he left.

THERAPY AND MIND CONTROL

Insight therapists strongly oppose the notion and practice of mind control. Their therapy is based on the idea that all behavioral change originates with the patients. The process of raising unconscious motives, emotions, and conflicts to the conscious level, they say, gives individuals control over their own mental processes and behavior patterns. The only mind control that successful insight therapy provides, they hold, is self-control. To this end, most therapists take great pains to avoid letting their own feelings, ideas, and beliefs influence their patients.

Critics, however, say that no therapist can be entirely objective and non-directive. Therapists are authority figures who control their patients much more than even they realize. Their patients or clients are usually troubled and feel somewhat helpless and dependent. Without being aware of it, many therapists unconsciously direct their patients' beliefs and values. Through questions, facial expressions, body movements, comments, or even sounds, they communicate approval or disapproval. To those with this point of view, then, insight therapy is a subtle and unplanned, but nonetheless significant, form of mind control.

CHAPTER 7.

BEHAVIOR MODIFICATION

Behavior Modification: A way to change
behavior through a plan of action by a therapist.
Often, a system of rewards and/or punishments
is used to strengthen wanted behavior and
weaken unwanted behavior.

Gail has just been promoted to the new position of
vice president in the bank where she works. She is
delighted with the promotion, but troubled too. The
job, Gail knows, involves a lot of travel by air around
the country. And Gail is deathly afraid of airplanes.
She has to overcome this fright quickly if she is to
handle the responsibilities of her new job. One of the
fastest ways to help Gail conquer her fear of flying is
through a method of treatment known as behavior
modification.

Gail was advised to see Dr. Gold, a psychologist

who specialized in behavior modification therapy. At the first session, Dr. Gold asked Gail to prepare a list of ten experiences, from the most relaxing (lying on a sunny beach) to the most frightening (going aboard an airplane). Then Dr. Gold taught Gail how to relax her body completely, from head to toe.

Once Gail was relaxed, Dr. Gold vividly described a day at the beach with Gail lying in the warm sun. Gail felt even calmer and more relaxed. Dr. Gold then moved on to the next experience on the list—listening to music. Again he described the situation in words while Gail imagined she was experiencing it. On and on he went. If Gail still felt relaxed, Dr. Gold went on to the next step. If she felt at all nervous, he backed up one step, so she could relax again.

In this way, over a series of eight sessions, Dr. Gold was able to get Gail to imagine entering the plane, being in her seat during take off, flying through the clouds, and landing—all without becoming tense. By the end of the treatment she was able to carry this confidence over to taking plane trips without any difficulty.

WHAT IS BEHAVIOR MODIFICATION?

Behavior modification is a step-by-step way of getting rid of unwanted patterns of thought or behavior, and putting in their place wanted or more desirable patterns.

In most ways, the techniques of behavior modification are quite different from those used in insight therapy. Behavior modification does not try to solve problems by uncovering the root causes of troubled behavior and bringing them to the conscious mind. Rather it holds that our ways of thinking and acting are the result of a process of learning. Therefore, getting rid of unwanted thoughts and actions must involve a process of unlearning the old ways.

OPERANT CONDITIONING

B. F. Skinner, professor of psychology at Harvard University, is a leader in the field of behavior modification. Skinner's methods of teaching people new ways to think and act are based, in part, on the experiments of the Russian scientist Ivan Pavlov (1849–1936), as well as the practical factory experiments of an American engineer, Frederick W. Taylor (1856–1915).

In Pavlov's most famous experiment, a bell was rung every time the laboratory dogs were fed. Dogs, just like humans, salivate when they see or smell food. After a number of repetitions, Pavlov just rang the bell, without feeding the dogs. He found that the dogs still salivated.

In this process of learning, called classical conditioning, a stimulus (ringing bell) that does not call forth a response (salivation) is paired with another stimulus (food), which does. The two stimuli are presented together a number of times. Eventually, the first stimulus (ringing the bell) alone produces the same response as the second (food).

Frederick Taylor's contribution was to break jobs down into their smallest separate tasks, and find the most efficient way to get each task done. His best-known research involved a laborer named Schmidt, who loaded heavy iron ingots into railroad cars in a steel mill. Taylor analyzed the steps of Schmidt's job, and figured out the best way to accomplish each one. The engineer then offered Schmidt a salary raise if he would do his job exactly as Taylor directed. The worker agreed. As a result, Schmidt increased his production by 400 percent. This cost Taylor only the promised 60 percent pay increase!

Skinner's method of bringing about new kinds of learning draws on the research of both Pavlov and Taylor. It is also based on two basic beliefs: One, that a person will repeat any act that is associated with a reward and avoid any act that is associated with punishment. Two, that complex patterns of behavior are learned gradually, step by step. Skinner's method is called operant conditioning.

Skinner's basic experiments with laboratory rats show operant conditioning at work. Suppose he wants to teach a rat to press a lever that is set in a wall of its cage. First, he makes sure that the rat is slightly hungry. Then, every time the rat comes near the wall with the lever, he rewards the rat with a pellet of food. After a while, he only gives the reward when the rat actually touches the wall. The next step is to provide food only when the rat touches the lever. Finally the rat must actually press the lever to earn the reward. In the end, the rat has learned to press the lever.

The teachers in an inner-city nursery program used operant conditioning to bring about changes in the behavior of a group of three- and four-year-olds who had poor verbal skills. When asked to tell what happened on the way to school or what they had had for breakfast, the children were apt to remain silent. The teachers decided to use Skinner's techniques to try to make the children more talkative.

The children's teachers carried packages of small candies in their pockets. Each time a child said a word, he or she would receive a candy; those who did not speak received nothing. After a while, the children found that they had to say entire sentences to earn a candy reward. In a few months, most of the children were speaking much more freely, even without the reward.

A form of operant conditioning called token economy is used in some mental hospitals and prisons. Patients or inmates earn tokens, which are usually coinlike plastic disks, for behaving in certain desired ways. Showering and brushing their teeth regularly, cooperating with the staff, helping to clean up, and preparing and serving the meals are some of the ways to earn tokens. The tokens are then traded in for extra favors or special privileges. At Alcoholics Anonymous, a self-help program for problem drinkers, members actually reward themselves with tokens if they go for a fixed length of time without a drink.

COUNTERCONDITIONING

Sometimes behavior is changed not by a system of rewards, as in operant conditioning, but by replacing one type of conduct with another. Called counterconditioning, it is one specific technique of behavior modification. Its goal usually is to substitute a desired response for one that is less desirable. An obese person's urge to eat candy is changed to disgust at the sight of sweets. A violinist who is nervous about performing in public learns to feel calm and relaxed onstage.

One approach to counterconditioning is based on negative reinforcement, which is also called aversive therapy. This may include an expression of disapproval by the therapist, withdrawal of privileges, or a mild electric shock. Thus, the person learns to associate the unpleasant experience with the unwanted behavior. And while the old behavior is fading out, a new way of acting is building up.

Some overweight individuals who seek help learn to change their eating habits and lose weight by aversive therapy. The overeaters are shown a series of pictures that include many high-calorie foods. Each time they look at a fattening food, they receive a mild, but painful, electric shock. When the picture changes to something healthful and nutritious, nothing happens. In time, the person in treatment begins to associate the pain of the shock with the fattening food. This association eventually becomes so strong that it overcomes the desire to eat foods that cause weight gain.

Slightly different from aversive therapy is a method in which overweight subjects are told to imagine their favorite fattening foods. At the same time, the therapist suggests some unsavory or disgusting association with that food. One person is told to imagine ants crawling on the slice of pizza he craves. Another is taught to think of worms on the inside of the chocolate bars she loves to devour. Once people build up these unpleasant thoughts about certain foods, they can't enjoy them anymore. As a result they lose weight. The same technique is used to treat alcoholics and smokers who want to break their habits.

Drugs have been tried in some counterconditioning experiments to change behavior. Apomorphine and anectine are two very powerful chemicals that have been given to violent or unruly prison inmates. Apomorphine causes severe vomiting; anectine relaxes the body's muscles, causing breathing to stop for several seconds. Prisoners who have been given these drugs say that the experiences are among the most frightening and painful they have ever endured. Critics hold that these drugs are more like punishments than methods of counterconditioning. Those who continue to use them, though, justify their use by claiming that they bring about desired changes in behavior.

SYSTEMATIC DESENSITIZATION

Some people have very strong, irrational fears. A young woman who is afraid of open spaces, a man who is afraid to go up in an elevator, or a child who cries at all loud sounds—these are some examples. Using a type of therapy called systematic desensitization, the therapist tries to erase the fear by reversing the learning process that made the person fearful in the first place. The object of fear is introduced, bit by bit, in a secure environment. Eventually the fearful feelings are replaced by calmness and control.

A classic story of desensitization has to do with a young boy named Peter. When Peter was a baby, he was startled by a loud noise while playing with a pet rabbit. As a result, he became afraid of the rabbit, and of all furry animals as well. The goal of Peter's desensitization treatment was to get rid of his fear of animals.

At first, Peter's therapist placed a caged rabbit in the same room as the boy, but far away from him. At the same time, she gave Peter some ice cream, which he particularly liked. The therapist repeated the experience over and over. An association began to form in Peter's mind between the ice cream and the rabbit. Each time, though, she brought the rabbit a little closer. Eventually, Peter built up such a pleasurable connection between the two objects that he was able to play with the rabbit again without any anxiety.

Various modern electronic measuring instruments are sometimes used with desensitization. These instruments note the most minute changes in heart rate, blood pressure, brain waves, muscle tension, or skin temperature. They also display the results for the individual to see in a technique known as biofeedback. Patients who are being treated for anxiety, for instance, may use biofeedback devices. They can watch a dial that shows their pulse rate increase or hear a tone that rises as their muscles tighten up. With this objective measure of the level of their anxiety, they can take an active role in the desensitization process.

Not long ago, a study reported some success in controlling severe migraine headaches using biofeedback techniques. Subjects in the experiment learned to control their blood circulation, thereby relieving some of the headache pain. In another experiment, a girl was trained to use biofeedback to control her brain waves. Every time she generated alpha waves, a particular pattern of electricity in the brain, a loudspeaker gave out a soft tone. In time, she found she could generate the alpha waves at will, which helped her to relax at times of great stress.

A QUESTION OF ETHICS

All the various types of therapy that have to do with behavior modification—operant conditioning, token economy, counterconditioning, aversive therapy, desensitization, and biofeedback—give some people a high degree of control over others.

These techniques seem to work best in situations where authority figures are in charge of others, such as in prisons and mental hospitals, as well as in factories and schools. The more power the prison officials, the mental hospital staff, the factory bosses, and schoolteachers have, the more effective is their ability to control others' thoughts and actions. Generally, also, the level of control is higher with children than with adults.

Many people are troubled by the prospect of widespread use of behavior modification. They ask: Is it ever morally correct for one person to use behavior modification to control the mind of another? Are there some situations where it is justified, and others where it is not? Should the techniques only be used on those who voluntarily seek help? Should they be used forcibly on anyone, such as a murderer or a rapist, who goes against society's most basic rules?

According to Professor Skinner, people have always tried to control the minds and actions of others. Throughout history, those who did not conform to society's rules were punished by torture, hanging, whipping, exile, prison, or some other way. Today's behavior modification techniques, he holds, are much more humane, successful, and scientific than those that were used long ago. And he believes that methods can eventually be developed to shape the behavior of entire nations, not only individuals, thereby creating a better life for everyone.

But not everyone accepts Professor Skinner's

views. Opponents believe that no one has the right to tamper with people's minds and behavior without their consent and approval. Every society has laws and punishments for those who break the law, they say, and that is protection enough. They believe that there is no justification for using behavior modification to change, against their own wills, the way people think and act in a free, democratic society.

CHAPTER 8.

HYPNOSIS

Hypnosis: An induced change of consciousness
that resembles sleep; hypnosis can make a
person more susceptible to suggestion.

In his laboratory filled with whirring computers and
bubbling chemicals in glass tubes, the evil scientist
stares deeply into the eyes of the young man tied to
a chair.

"Now, you are in my power," the scientist says.
"And tonight you *kill!*"

Suddenly the scene shifts. The young man, walking
stiffly and with glazed eyes, breaks into a darkened
house. He enters the room of a beautiful woman who
is asleep in her bed. As she awakens and starts to
scream, the man attacks, and chokes her to death.

Such fictional descriptions of hypnosis are found in
many books and movies. Interesting as they may be,

they are very different from hypnosis in real life. Doctors consider hypnosis a valuable tool for treating a number of mental and physical ills. Scientists also believe it has an important part to play in unraveling the mysteries of the human mind. And even the police sometimes use hypnosis to help them solve crimes.

WHAT IS HYPNOSIS?

Trained therapists can use the power of hypnosis to control thought, influence emotions, and speed up or slow down body processes. Through hypnosis, they can help people recall repressed memories, relieve fears and anxieties, reduce pain, change attitudes, and bring about alterations in breathing, blood pressure, or electrical brain activity.

Experts estimate that about 95 percent of the population can be hypnotized. Included in this very large group are the young and old, bright and dull, well-educated and illiterate, shy and outgoing, anxious and calm, emotionally disturbed and well-adjusted. Only a prejudice against hypnotism seems likely to affect success.

The actual process of hypnosis is quite simple. Before starting, though, many hypnotists give the subject a quick test. They might ask the subject to clasp hands tightly together. With the hands thus locked in position, the hypnotists say, "Your hands cannot be separated. You cannot pull them apart." People whose hands remain locked, or who can separate them only with difficulty, are considered apt to make good subjects.

In the usual voice method of hypnosis, the subject sits in a comfortable chair. The hypnotist, in a confident and soothing manner, tells the individual to relax. Talking in the same quiet tone of voice, the hypnotist may make suggestions: "Empty your mind of all thoughts. Give in to your tiredness. Allow sleep to take over."

Many subjects' eyes begin to flutter and close within a few moments. The hypnotist then urges a deeper sleep. Soon everything is blotted out for the subject except the sound of the hypnotist's voice.

Sometimes, in addition to the use of the voice, the hypnotist will suggest a point of focus for the subject to stare at. The point may be a small shiny object, like a key or ring, a source of dim light, such as a candle flame, or a spot on a blank wall. The focal point is almost always above the person's line of vision, forcing him or her to look up. While the subject stares at the point, the hypnotist urges the individual to force out all other thoughts and concentrate only on the object.

When the person appears to be entering the hypnotic state, the hypnotist may command him or her to carry out an order. This test measures the depth of the hypnosis.

"Hold your right arm straight out," the hypnotist says. "It is very stiff. You cannot bend it."

Then the hypnotist orders the subject to bend the arm. If the subject tries to bend it, but cannot, the hypnotist knows the person has entered the hypnotic state.

At the end, subjects are brought out of the hypnotic state in one of two ways. Most often the hypnotist tells the person that he or she will wake up at the count of ten. By the time the operator has finished the slow count, the subject is fully awake. Sometimes the hypnotist ends the trance by ceasing to make voice contact with the person. Gradually, then, the individual either wakes up or falls into a normal sleep.

THE HYPNOTIC STATE

The single most outstanding feature of the hypnotic state is the subject's willingness to accept suggestions from the hypnotist. Stage hypnotists demonstrate this in any number of ways.

"It is freezing cold," the hypnotist says. At once, the subjects start to shiver and pull their clothes tightly around them, no matter the temperature.

The hypnotist suggests to the subjects that they

are dogs. Soon everyone is jumping around on all fours, and barking loudly.

The hypnotist tells someone his body is as stiff as a board. That person can now be balanced with feet on one chair and head on another—without sagging in the middle!

While stage hypnotists use hypnosis for entertainment, many doctors find it a valuable treatment tool. One evening, a dazed teen-aged girl was found wandering the streets of Chicago. The police tried to find out what had happened. But the girl was unable—or unwilling—to tell them. A psychologist who specialized in hypnotism was called in to try to help.

Once she was under hypnosis, he urged her to recall what had happened. It took some time, but bit by bit she told the following story: She had come home from school as usual that afternoon. When she got to the apartment, no one answered the doorbell. She thought her mother was out, so she unlocked the door and walked toward the kitchen for a snack. As she passed the bedroom, she saw her parents sprawled out on the bed. They were both dead. The empty pill bottles on the floor told her that they had committed suicide. The girl tried to call the police, but found that she could not speak. Her head in a fog, she went out and started wandering the streets.

The psychologist arranged daily therapy sessions

with the girl. He spoke to her each time, even though she did not answer. He also hypnotized her, and helped her to relive the tragedy so she could understand and accept what had happened.

After weeks of treatment, the girl began to speak again. Despite stretches of depression and apathy, as well as daily crying spells, she began to pull her life together. After a year, she still has terrible nightmares. But everyone hopes she is on the road to recovery.

Hypnosis can also be used to bring about direct changes in behavior. It can be used during childbirth so that the mother does not need to be given an anesthetic. Sometimes surgery can be performed with only hypnosis to control the pain. A young man was once able to work comfortably in 104-degree heat by the hypnotic suggestion that he recall swimming in the cool ocean.

Hypnotists can also bring about sharp changes in drive and motivation. A middle-aged widow was depressed and apathetic because of her emotional problems. She found it hard to do her chores—even to move around the house. By planting hypnotic suggestions in her mind—"You will get out of bed every morning and get dressed. You will make breakfast and eat it. After breakfast, you will clean the house and make the bed."—and so on, the hypnotist restored her to normal levels of activity.

In the hands of a skilled hypnotist, suggestions made while the subject is in the hypnotic state can be extended to the normal waking state. This is called posthypnotic suggestion. Let's say a heavy smoker wants to break his smoking habit. After placing him in a hypnotic trance, the hypnotist tells the subject that after waking, cigarettes will taste like burning rubber. Further, he instructs him to forget the source of the suggestion.

After coming out of the trance, the subject lights a cigarette. Sure enough, the cigarette tastes and smells like a burning tire. He tries cigarette after cigarette. One is worse than the other. Although he does not know why, he just gives up the habit, and stops smoking. And since the memory of the hypnotic suggestion is gone, the man thinks it was his own idea to stop smoking.

Posthypnotic suggestion is also used to treat insomnia, speech disorders, nightmares, shyness, and many fears and phobias as well as addiction to nicotine, drugs, or alcohol. Sometimes hypnotic control can cure a medical condition that has no physical basis.

The police frequently put hypnosis to work in solving crimes. In July 1976, for example, three masked men in a van kidnapped a busload of children and their driver. They hid the hostages in a trailer-truck that was buried underground. Eventually the driver and children were rescued. When questioned, the school-bus driver was unable to remember anything about the van. Under hypnosis, however, he was able to recall most of the van's license plate number. It was enough of a lead to solve the case.

THEORIES OF HYPNOTISM

Although hypnotism is an old and much-studied technique, no one is quite sure what it is or how it works. Experts know that it brings about some changes in the electrical and chemical activity of the brain that are different from the activity of either the sleeping or the wakeful state. But the exact nature of these changes is not known. The best guess seems to be that placing the individual in a calm, relaxed state reduces the stress on the brain. Then, presumably, something happens that allows the brain to continue functioning, while accepting suggestions at the same time.

One of the earliest theories of hypnosis was that it was a magnetic force that flowed from the hypnotist into the subject. During the eighteenth century, the Austrian doctor Franz Anton Mesmer (1734–1815) was able to hypnotize people, and cure their illnesses, by touching them with his "magical" magnetic wand.

The once-popular theory that hypnosis is a form of sleep is now also discredited. Sleep and hypnosis may look alike, but laboratory studies show that they are quite different. In fact, during hypnosis some important functions, such as heartbeat, breathing, and body movements, are more like what is found in the waking state than while asleep.

Everyone agrees that suggestion plays a big role in hypnosis. That is, the subject tends to accept directions from the hypnotist. Some say that hypnosis is the direct result of suggestion. Others feel it comes about indirectly, by suppressing a person's conscious thoughts and will. Still another theory holds that hypnosis splits off parts of the human mind from the main stream of consciousness. The split part acts independently and may actually begin to control the person.

Certain psychiatrists say that the success of hypnotism has more to do with a person's wish to be hypnotized than anything else. The need some people feel to submit their will to another may also be a factor. According to a Freudian belief, hypnotism can allow subjects to return to the childlike state to become aware of repressed, or buried, emotions.

Finally, there is the notion that hypnotized subjects act or play out a game according to what they think is expected of them. They act helpless, silly, or forgetful, depending on what they believe the hypnotist wants. Certain evidence to the contrary, however, indicates that subjects often do not act in expected ways at all.

FOR BETTER OR WORSE

In some ways, hypnosis is like a powerful drug. If used correctly, it can be of benefit to the subject. But used improperly, it can cause harm. Trained doctors, and even stage hypnotists, mostly use hypnotism without danger. But the risks for people who do not really understand hypnotism, and do not know what happens to the subject during the trance, can be considerable.

Many people object to hypnosis because they believe it gives one person almost complete control over another. The hypnotist can, if desired, cause moral, psychological, or physical harm to the subject. They say that the process really makes individuals surrender their will and awareness, so that they are more liable to be injured.

The moral harm comes if subjects are forced to commit acts that they would not ordinarily do if they were awake. There may be psychological damage if the subjects do not want to be hypnotized, or are not aware that they are undergoing hypnosis. Also, if the hypnotist is not careful, subjects may carry certain frightening hallucinations from their hypnotic experience over into the waking state.

Hypnotists may also abuse subjects in ways that result in physical injury. In one dramatic experiment performed at the University of Tulsa, Oklahoma, hypnotized subjects were urged to reach into a case containing live rattlesnakes. The subjects were starting to carry out the order when they were stopped. The conclusion was that people in deep hypnosis will sometimes commit dangerous acts if they are so directed.

Most experts now agree, however, that there are limits to what people will or will not do under hypnosis. It is unusual for individuals to commit an act they really consider immoral or offensive. While in the hypnotic state, an honest person will not usually tell a lie, a normally modest person is not likely to undress, and a moral person is not apt to commit a crime.

CHAPTER 9.

BRAIN MANIPULATION

Brain Manipulation: Attempts to alter behavior
by applying electrical current to the brain, or by
destroying parts of the brain by surgery.

The hope of controlling behavior or curing mental
disease by reaching directly into the brain has existed
for many centuries. Holes in the skulls of skeletons
dating back thousands of years indicate that many
such efforts were made in the distant past. But it was
not until the twentieth century that a scientific basis
for brain manipulation was established. From this research three current approaches to brain manipulation have evolved: electric shock treatment, electrical
stimulation of the brain, and psychosurgery.

ELECTRIC SHOCK TREATMENT

Electric shock treatment is the common name for electroconvulsive therapy, or ECT. ECT is used by doctors to relieve cases of severe depression or extreme hyperactivity. The technique is to send a current of electricity through the brain, resulting in convulsions and a brief loss of consciousness.

Many psychiatrists consider ECT an effective treatment for certain serious mental conditions. It is, therefore, used in about 90 percent of the mental hospitals in the United States. Critics, however, insist that it is no more than a torture device used to control and manage uncooperative or unruly mental patients.

In the modern use of ECT, the patient is given a tranquilizer or sedative before treatment. This calms the patient and relieves any anxiety. Next the patient is given a general anesthetic and a muscle relaxant. The anesthetic eliminates pain; the relaxant prevents violent convulsions and injuries that might result. Throughout the procedure, too, the patient receives oxygen. This lessens some of the bad side effects that are due to brief interruptions in breathing.

A physician administers the actual shock by holding two large electrodes at either side of the patient's temples. For around one second, between 500 and 900 milliamperes flow through the person's brain. This is about as much current as is used to light a 100-watt lightbulb. No one knows the exact effect of this electricity. But the patient's muscles twitch and stiffen, and then he or she falls into a deep sleep.

One of the biggest problems with ECT is that it impairs the memories of those receiving the treatment. The great American writer Ernest Hemingway, for instance, received ECT for his depression. He later insisted that the treatment had destroyed him as an author. "What is the sense of ruining my head and erasing my memory, which is my capital, and putting me out of business? It was a brilliant cure but we lost the patient," he wrote just before ending his life by suicide.

Many depressed patients, though, depend on ECT to control their condition. Without the treatment, most would be unable to function. Several might attempt suicide. ECT is also useful for those who do not respond well to antidepressant drugs, or who suffer unusual side effects from these medicines.

Nonetheless, emotions run very strongly against the use of ECT. In Berkeley, California, 61 percent of the voters in the November 1982 election passed a law banning the use of ECT in the city. Just two months later, though, a court overturned the law. The judge ruled the new law illegal because there was already a state law regulating ECT.

Most people who oppose ECT fear that it is being used more to control human behavior than as therapy for the mentally ill. The magazine *Psychiatric News* carried a report a few years ago detailing numerous instances of ECT misuse. Two former mental-hospital workers told of ECT treatments that were administered improperly. Instead of being used only on depressed or hyperactive patients, they were given to a female alcoholic, an abused wife who attacked her husband, a seventy-year-old man who was recently forced to move from his home, and a severely mentally retarded twenty-six-year-old who was difficult to handle in the hospital.

Perhaps the most notorious example of the use of ECT to control behavior rather than to treat mental illness took place at the Bien Hoa Hospital in Vietnam during the summer of 1966. Dr. Lloyd Cotter, a psychiatrist from Pomona, California, was in charge of the crowded hospital. He wanted to start a program in which a group of severely disturbed male patients would work on the hospital grounds as preparation for being discharged. Many refused. Those who said no to the plan were given a series of three ECTs a week. Gradually, more and more of these patients agreed to work. The doctor credited his success partly to the effects of the treatments, and partly to the dislike or fear of the ECTs. Most observers see the change in behavior simply as a dread of further treatment.

ELECTRICAL STIMULATION OF THE BRAIN

A man stood alone in the center of a giant bullring in Madrid, Spain. Opposite him stood a big, powerful bull, one bred to attack in a bullfight. The man waved a matador's red cape. The bull lowered its head and charged at full speed. When the bull was but four feet away, the man pulled a miniature radio transmitter from his pocket and pushed a button. In an instant, the bull stopped, turned, and started to walk in a circle, completely ignoring the man.

The confident man in the bullring was Dr. José Delgado, a leading researcher in the field of electrical stimulation of the brain, also known as ESB. Earlier, Dr. Delgado had implanted a number of wire-thin electrodes in the bull's brain. The wires were connected to a miniature radio receiver which he had placed beneath the skin of the animal's head. When Dr. Delgado pushed the button on his radio transmitter, it sent a mild electric current into the bull's brain. By stimulating the bull's brain, Dr. Delgado was able to control the animal's aggression and make it calm and placid.

In the 1920s, a Swiss researcher, Walter R. Hess, found that by electrically stimulating one particular part of a cat's brain, the hypothalamus, he could change the cat's behavior. With a flip of a switch, for example, he could turn good-natured cats into raging, attacking, bad-tempered animals.

Since then, some research has been concerned with mapping the brain, much as astronomers map the sky. These scientists, working with lab animals, stimulate different parts of the brain and observe the reactions. They are learning how to control the mind to a remarkable degree. By stimulating one point they can create fearful behavior; at another point they call forth angry actions. In the same way, they have found the pleasure and pain centers, the sites of sexual desire and of hunger. They can, in their labs, make the animals relaxed or tense, active or sedate, and so on.

Dr. Delgado and others have tried to find human applications for this form of mind control. In one case, a young man, whose left arm was paralyzed as a result of an auto accident, suffered continual pain. Doctors prescribed many different drugs and tried various forms of physical therapy, but none offered him any relief. As a result of the constant pain, the man's personality changed, and he became hostile and bitter.

Dr. Delgado suggested using ESB to ease the condition. He implanted an electrode in the man's brain and connected it to a stimulator that he placed under the scalp. The subject had a switch to turn on the electricity whenever he felt the pain starting. The electrical stimulation provided relief. Within a year his behavior had returned to normal.

Scientists can also curb violent outbursts of temper by means of ESB. They can lead normally silent people to become chatty, calm down those who may be overactive, and energize the depressed. Some patients have become so friendly under ESB that they even tried to kiss the doctor and have proposed marriage!

The latest ESB device designed by Dr. Delgado is called a stimoceiver. It contains a tiny computer chip and four electrodes that extend from the scalp down into the brain. The electrodes pick up changes of electrical activity within the brain that signal pain or a problem of some kind. Automatically the computer chip gets the message, and sends out the proper electrical stimulation to control the difficulty. With other devices, either the patients can operate the stimulator at will, or a doctor can do it via radio waves from a distance.

Dr. Robert G. Heath of Tulane University has located a pleasure center within the brain. When stimulated, it gives the patient strong feelings of satisfaction. The stimulator is completely under the control of the user. Built with an automatic counter, it keeps a record of the number of times it is used. In one experiment, a patient stimulated himself one thousand times in just one hour! During the 1960s, Dr. Heath used this form of ESB to treat patients with various mental illnesses. He also treated a number of homosexuals who wanted to change their sexual preference.

ESB has many critics who object to its use for many reasons. They argue that further development of ESB may one day allow an all-powerful government to establish control over the entire population. By implanting electrodes in everyone's brain and broadcasting certain radio signals, that government would be able to direct the thinking and behavior of every citizen.

Also, many distrust the experimental results. They claim that there is no real proof that ESB is effective. Take the case of the charging bull. Dr. Delgado has written that the stimulation changed the mood of the bull. Opponents say that he merely paralyzed some of the bull's muscles—thus stopping the animal's advance. They wonder if the attacks of temper and violence brought on by ESB are anything more than ordinary reactions to pain caused by the stimulation.

Few scientists have been able to repeat the experiments and obtain the same results as the few well-known ESB researchers. Before the scientific community can accept a new idea, other scientists must be able to perform the same experiments and get similar findings.

We are now at a crossroads in the development of ESB. Scientists can confine its use mostly to laboratory research on mapping the brain and learning the functions of the different parts of the brain. Or they can extend and apply the findings to find ways of shaping behavior and personality in human individuals. Dr. Delgado suggests this latter application: "The question is no longer 'What is man?'; it has now become 'What kind of man are we going to construct?' "

PSYCHOSURGERY

Over the years, there have been many attempts to cure severe mental illness with surgery on the brain, a treatment known as psychosurgery. The idea grew from the old notion that mental illness springs from damaged brain cells, just as many physical illnesses result from defective body cells. According to this belief, the way to cure mental illness is by cutting away or destroying these harmful cells.

In 1935 Dr. Egas Moniz (1874–1955) in Lisbon, Portugal, carried out the first modern version of this type of operation. He drilled a small hole through the patient's temple, and removed tiny bits of tissue from the front lobe of the brain. He did this operation on a number of severely disturbed violent mental patients and reported remarkable improvements in their conditions and behaviors. For his work in psychosurgery Moniz was awarded the 1949 Nobel Prize in Medicine. An unfortunate footnote, however, is that one of the patients Moniz pronounced considerably improved as a result of surgery later shot the doctor, leaving him permanently paralyzed.

Dr. Walter Freeman carried Dr. Moniz's work forward in the United States. Freeman devised a faster, easier way to enter the brain. His technique was to insert a sharp instrument, like an ice pick, into the brain through the soft tissue above the eyeball and under the eyelid. He then used a back-and-forth type motion, like a windshield wiper, to cut some of the nerve pathways in the brain. Since these nerves go to the prefrontal lobes, the operation is known as a prefrontal lobotomy.

It took Dr. Freeman but a few minutes to perform a prefrontal lobotomy. He claimed to have performed the operation on 3,500 patients from the mid 1930s until the 1950s. In a demonstration at a Virginia mental hospital in 1948, Dr. Freeman completed eight prefrontal lobotomies in just one afternoon. For the climax he did two operations at the same time, using two picks simultaneously! By 1950, over 100,000 of these surgical procedures had been done worldwide.

The early reports by surgeons who used this method were quite good. Most claimed success in curbing violence and putting an end to wide emotional swings, as well as reducing anxiety and tension in their patients. It soon became apparent, though, that there were other far less desirable changes in personality and mental functioning. Patients who had lobotomies suffered a drop in energy and often lost their ability to respond emotionally. Many showed diminished learning or memory skills, along with such behaviors as a lack of concern for their appearance, hyperactivity, overeating, and strangely enough, the use of crude and abusive language.

With the introduction of tranquilizers in the 1950s, and the growing awareness of the disastrous side effects of psychosurgery, activity in this area fell off sharply. Only about ten surgeons in the United States still perform prefrontal lobotomies. Usually, they do the operation only on very violent or severely disturbed patients who cannot be helped in any other way. An estimated five hundred to one thousand of these operations are still done each year.

The most common modern psychosurgery technique is known as stereotaxis. X rays and a metal frame placed over the patient's head are used to guide the insertion of thin wire electrodes to specific points within the brain. The doctor then uses the electrodes to monitor the brain waves at these points.

Sometimes a weak electrical current is fed through the electrode, and any changes in the patient's behavior are noted. If out-of-the-ordinary brain waves are picked up at any point, or if the electrical stimulation produces unusual behavior, a powerful charge of electricity is sent through the electrode, destroying the adjacent brain cells.

The outcomes of modern stereotaxic psychosurgery are uncertain at best. The reported results range from control of the symptoms of severe disorders to total deterioration of functioning. One "overactive, aggressive, destructive" nine-year-old boy in Mississippi not long ago underwent four stereotaxic operations. In addition to becoming dull and robotlike, the patient's IQ dropped from 115 to 60.

Today's use of psychosurgery is mostly confined to mental hospitals. Some advocates, though, suggest its use in prisons. Hardened offenders, they say, should be given the choice of being released after having their criminal behavior eliminated by psychosurgery, or of serving their full terms in jail. They hold that it is more humane to control destructive thoughts and behavior with psychosurgery than through a lifetime behind bars.

Opponents, though, strongly object to this extreme application of mind and behavior control. They point out that the brain damage caused by the operation can never be repaired. And after surgery, some patients suffer so much mental and emotional loss that they can best be described as "zombies" or "vegetables." In response to these concerns some countries, such as the Soviet Union, have completely banned psychosurgery. And in most other countries, it is limited to only those mental patients for whom all other treatment methods have failed.

In summary, mind control is a widespread and varied phenomenon. It is accomplished in many different ways—from applying group pressure to destroying part of the brain, from fasting to hypnosis. Sometimes people set out to control their own thoughts—as by entering an altered state or taking illicit drugs. More often the mind-control techniques are applied by others—as in cult conversion or behavior modification. The motives behind the use of mind control also range widely—from treating mental disease with insight therapy to robbing people of their beliefs through brainwashing.

Because of the breadth and depth of mind control, it is a difficult subject about which to generalize. All that can be truly said is that it is very much part of our modern world. Its use and effectiveness are both rapidly growing. For these reasons, it is vitally important that every one of us monitor its spread. Only in this way can we protect ourselves from the dangers of mind control, while enjoying any benefits that it can provide.

FOR FURTHER READING

Appel, Willa. *Cults in America: Programmed for Paradise.* New York: Holt, Rinehart & Winston, 1983.

Blythe, Peter. *Hypnotism: Its Power and Practice.* New York: Taplinger, 1971.

Chavkin, Samuel. *The Mind Stealers.* Boston: Houghton Mifflin, 1978.

Edwin, B. *Psycho-Yoga: The Practice of Mind Control.* New York: Citadel, 1969.

Hanna, David. *Cults in America.* New York: Tower, 1979.

Hunter, Edward. *Brainwashing.* New York: Farrar, Straus & Cudahy, 1956.

Lifton, Robert Jay. *Thought Reform and the Psychology of Totalism.* New York: W. W. Norton, 1969.

Lilly, John C. *The Center of the Cyclone: An Autobiography of Inner Space.* New York: Bantam, 1972.

Meerloo, J.A.M. *The Rape of the Mind.* Cleveland: World, 1956.

Mills, Jeannie. *Six Years with God.* New York: A & W, 1979.

Pines, Maya. *The Brain Changers: Scientists and the New Mind Control.* New York: Harcourt Brace Jovanovich, 1973.

Rhodes, Raphael H. *Hypnosis: Theory, Practice and Application.* New York: Citadel, 1960.

Rudin, James A. and Marcia R. *Prison or Paradise? The New Religious Cults.* Philadelphia: Fortress, 1980.

Sargant, William. *Battle for the Mind.* Garden City, New York: Doubleday, 1957.

Scheflin, Alan W. and Edward M. Opton, Jr. *The Mind Manipulators.* New York: Paddington, 1978.

Schein, Edgar. *Coercive Persuasion.* New York: W. W. Norton, 1961.

Schrag, Peter. *Mind Control.* New York: Pantheon, 1978.

Shutts, David. *Lobotomy: Resort to the Knife.* New York: Van Nostrand Reinhold, 1982.

Stoner, Carroll and Jo Anne Parke. *All God's Children: The Cult Experience—Salvation or Slavery?* Philadelphia: Chilton, 1977.

Streiker, Lowell D. *Cults: The Continuing Threat.* Nashville, Tennessee: Abingdon, 1983.

Underwood, Barbara and Betty. *Hostage to Heaven.* New York: Clarkson N. Potter, 1979.

Valenstein, Elliot S. *Brain Control: A Critical Examination of Brain Stimulation and Psychosurgery.* New York: John Wiley & Sons, 1973.

Valenstein, Elliot S., editor. *The Psychosurgery Debate: Scientific, Legal and Ethical Perspectives.* New York: W. H. Freeman, 1980.

White, John, editor. *The Highest State of Consciousness.* Garden City, New York: Anchor, 1972.

Yee, Min S. and Thomas N. Layton. *In My Father's House.* New York: Holt, Rinehart & Winston, 1981.

INDEX

addiction, 42, 45, 46, 47
alcohol, 5–6, 8, 42–44, 45
Alcoholics Anonymous, 75
alpha waves, 79
altered states, 48–61, 105
    definition, 48, 49–51
Altered States of
    Consciousness Induction
    Device (ASCID), 59–60
amphetamines, 46
Amytal, 45
Anectine, 77
anesthetic, 94
antidepressant drugs, 38, 95
antimanic drugs, 38
antipsychotic drugs, 37–39, 47
Apomorphine, 77
Artemis Orthia temple, 60

asanas, 52
ASCID, 59–60
aversive therapy, 76, 79

Barbital, 45
barbiturates, 45
behavior modification, 5–6,
    70–81, 105
    definition, 70, 71–72
    techniques, 72
Bible, 56
Bien Hoa Hospital (Vietnam),
    96–97
Big Brother, 9
biofeedback, 78–79
blood-alcohol level, 43
blood pressure, 78
body discipline, 54–56